THIS
IS
NOT
ANOTHER
LOVE
SONG

a collection of poetry, prose and poem stories

BY

N'KYENGE AYANNA

DEDICATION

I dedicate this book to my mother Frances, mi Roca, mi Corazon y mi amiga mejor who consistently encourages me and has always demonstrated persistence in reminding me of who I am, who I belong too and that my dreams are limitless. I love you so much Mom! Delay is not denial, not ever!

I also dedicate this book to my big sister, Latasha, who left us way too soon and was very instrumental in pushing me to get my book(s) published! I am keeping a promise I made to her before she went to Heaven. Sis, I can feel your celebration and praise, I love you forever girl!

Synopsis

A multi-voiced chapbook featuring nine powerful
and passionate women speaking their truths about
L.O.V.E
9 women unbeknownst to each other
9 voices accented and accentuated
9 exceptionally different expressions of love
Spoken then shaped in sound

"THIS IS NOT ANOTHER LOVE SONG"

Table of Contents

CH. 1
In the beginning

Was love until love wasn't enough. I never could tell when
you were lying so you thought and you, you were my ace,
my very best friend so I thought, and we are miles away
from forgetting.

I am femininity, Goddess sun and Negro Black, I am every
moment of this skin and I have memorized your hands
wrapped around my thighs, your head tilted, I
Turn the lights out and wait for you to come every night

You don't call
That much anymore, every now and then I get a mediocre
response to an email after I talked myself out of writing
you and then right back into "checking" on you because
that's who I am and I hate that you make me feel like I
can't get you out of me, I hate that I wake up sometimes
with panties soaked from your memory
YOU ARE THE ITCH IN MY SKIN

my best friend, my companion, my man, you were my man
my understanding
the only way I knew how to live
the only way I knew how to love
I can't grove like I used to
I'm weightless without you
I haven't learned to care less about you
Not sure how to be without you because

I remember how you would slowly suck the lobe of my ear
The way you nibbled and kissed it slow-ly, the soft
whispers I love you forever and tomorrow and the next
I WILL NOT BE LOST WITHOUT YOU!

I will snatch my second wind and fly damnit!
You misunderstood my strength
You mistook my voice for blind reprimand and
Not for the instrument it is and was meant to be
I played for you a symphony
I sang a tune of acquiesce
La La La and baby, I forgive you, damn I for-give

The last time was the last time I let you make love to my
mind and never mind my body
I have to, so I forgive you
I don't want to lose my soul
I know that I can be whole
Without you
I'm not lost without you
I'm so very happy without you
In the end

GENESIS: I AM "THE BEGINNING"

This is Not Another Love Song

CH.2

drum roll, again and again and one mo' again

I CAN'T BREATHE, POUNDING IN MY EAR, THERE
IS POUNDING IN MY EAR I FEEL LIKE I'M
STROKING OUT, I'M HAVING A HEART ATTACK
MAYBE WHAT DO YOU MEAN IT AIN'T YOUR
BABY! HOW COULD YOU SAY THIS IS NOT YOUR
BABY?

REMEMBER
YOU CALLED ME BABY, SAID I WAS FOREVER
YOUR BABY, YOU TOOK MY VIRGINITY, YOU
KNOW THAT BECAUSE YOU WIPED THE BLOOD
AWAYHUSHED AWAY MY TEARSGRINDED AWAY
MY FEARS, YOUBUSTED MY HYMAN YOU'RE
YOUR ERECTION

KISSED
AWAY THE HURT WITH PERFECTION SCRIPTED,
YOU WERE MY MASTER IN TOO MANY WAYS YOU
TOWERED OVER ME WITH YOUR LOVENOT
HARMING BUT HURTING ME WITH YOUR LOVE
SILHOUETTE SHADOWS ON THE WALL

YOU
WALKED AWAY IN THE MIDDLE OF THE NIGHT
MY BELLY SWOLLEN ANGER SOAKED SKIN, I
CAN'T BELIEVE WE'RE GOING THROUGH THIS ISH
AGAIN

SEND
ME THE TEST RESULTS YOU SHOUTED AS YOU
STORMED DOWN THE STAIRS THIS MAN DOESN'T
EVEN CARE HOW CAN HE NOT CARE?
WHY DON'T YOU CARE?

8

WHY
YOU ACTIN' LIKE THIS, I ASKED YOU ON THE
PHONE, YOU SAID YOU DIDN'T WANT TO DISCUSS
IT LEAVE ME

ALONE
ALONE IN MY ROOM SOMETIMES I STARE AT THE
WALL AND IN THE BACK OF MY MIND I HEAR MY
CONSCIOUS CALL, I'M BANGIN **L.L** RIGHT NOW,
I'M RIPPING UP SHIT THINKING ABOUT OUR LAST
TALK, I'M CALMING MYSELF DOWN BECAUSE I'M
GONE BE ALRIGHT I GOT MUSIC IN MY SOUL,
GONNA ROCK ITUNES ALL NIGHT AND WHEN I
WAKE UP

WHEN
I WAKE UP TOMORROW WITH SWOLLEN EYES
AND A 7MONTH BELLY TO MATCH I WILL LIGHT
A CANDLE, WALK THE BEACH BAREFOOT AND
DRIFT YOU INTO THE OCEAN DEEP
I'M A SOLDIER OF LOVE, BUT YOU ALREADY
KNEW

THAT
I'M
IZABELLA SADE
I WAS MADE TO MOVE MOUNTAINS
PLANTED MUSTARD SEEDS ALL AROUND ME
GREW A GARDEN OF PLENTY ALL BY FAITH
ME AND MY BABY GONE' BE ALRIGHT
SELAH~

I'M IZABELLA: (DEVOTED TO GOD), YOU CAN CALL
ME IZA (E-SAH)

Ch.3
chocolate sun

THERE IS LOVE
THERE IS LOVE IN YOUR EYES
I CAN SEE IT IN MY DREAMS
I FEEL IT WHEN YOU SPEAK
AND MY HEART SAYS
TRUST HIM GIRL
THIS TIME IT'S FOR REAL
THERE IS LOVE

I wanted every part of you. Sunrise to sunset. I remember the ocean the day after we met, the way the waves tickled all over and the sand gushed between my toes molding me into another world. That's how it feels when I am with you. Saxophone and flute we are two very different instruments that play the same tune once the fingers are placed correctly. I am a black mermaid with scales and scars and skin like tar I am a rare pearl. I am Africa and Brazil I am something you can feel deeply in your soul, you said that on the third day. We are a trio on repeat.

Me, you, love.
Love, you, I.
You love me.
I love you. I love you, I do and
THERE IS LOVE
THERE IS LOVE, IN YOUR EYES
I CAN SEE IT IN MY DREAMS
I FEEL IT WHEN YOU SPEAK
AND MY HEART SAYS
TRUST HIM GIRL
THIS TIME IT'S FOR REAL
THERE
IS
LOVE

I fade into this day. I melt into this sunshine. What if I let myself love you? If even for a moment I could set myself free. I could lose these solidarity chains that bind me, that keep me from the unforeseen, the not planned. With us, everything is happenstance
> and
>> we
>>> concede
>>>> circumstance.

I'M MICAELA: (Me-ky-A-yah) AND MY NAME MEANS "WHO IS LIKE GOD"

CH.4
when the bass hits the spot

To the tick-tock and you don't stop
Yo the hip-hop makes my body rock
To the bang-bang boogie that up jumps the boogie
I am boogie oogie like midnight sky
You said you wanted love there is none greater than I
They call me Kaeana (Kay-ah-nah)
Black daughter of Ghana
Hey, oh My name means praised
Hey, oh every single hand raised

So, this morning I watched the sun come up
I don't know why, I just did, and I played like my life was
different and things went the way I planned exactly, and I
followed my own direction
Went down the right path, but when the
light split between the trees and the sun began to speak
I felt like I was free
And once again life mattered to me
And the birds crooned
I was doing my own thing and
On my left hand there was a wedding ring
Then my soul pleaded to sing
Everybody loves the sunshine
But when it's dark outside
Like it is right now
I see darkness
And it's not just because my eyes are closed
Or my mirror image is too black to look back
Tell me what is too much to expect, I
Feel what I feel when I feel what I feel when I'm feeling
I am exhausted with nonchalant emptiness
I Can't stop looking at the time, my
Fingers shake as I try to press rewind

To the tick-tock and you don't stop
Yo the hip-hop makes my body rock
To the bang-bang boogie that up jumps the boogie
I am boogie oogie like midnight sky
You said you wanted love there is none greater than I
They call me Kaeana (Kay-ah-nah)
Black daughter of Ghana
Hey, oh My name means praised
Hey, oh every single hand raised

I don't even know
What I'm waiting on
I don't even know
What I'm looking for
Anymore
Anymore

Something feels different, something feels strangely surreal
Hoping this time, he gives me something I can feel
Want the anxiety to cease
Want to catch and release
Want my afflictions to decease
Ticka-tah Ticka -tah Ticka tah-tah -tah
Gotta give me something to croon too
Said I was your sun and you were my moon
Life is a cocktail, continue the groove

I AM KA'ENA: MY NAME MEANS" PRAISED"

CH.5
Makin' love in the kitchen

I made you curried chicken from Trinidad & Tobago it was
from scratch and my Mama's recipe. It took many hours,
but it was cooked with love because of the way I love you,
I prepared rainbow cabbage with a trio of peppers, made
maple-gingered-cinnamon carrots, sweet plantains and
garlic roti. I didn't order it from a restaurant or defrost it
from a store-bought box. Instead, I spent countless hours,
chopping, cutting, sautéing, marinating, waiting, Waiting
and waiting but you didn't show up, you didn't call, didn't
text, didn't nothing. Where the hell are you?

I set the table, decorated it with shiny china and silk
napkins that made the silver ware look so very sexy, so
very sexy was I in my Ice Cream Lady black "Leopard on
the Loose" couture fish-nets. I was hosed to perfection, my
yum-yum mix blazed through the Bluetooth speakers Sade,
Jill Scott, Floetry, Maxwell, The Isley Brothers, Jodeci, and
Sade again, but when she started singing softly Somebody
Already Broke My Heart, I broke all the way down, then

I glossed my lips tried to turn my mind off, his phone is dead
I said as I sprayed Le Baiser du Dragon perfuming my neck,
wrists and thighs. Put on my Fuscia pumps, painted Fuscia
lips, hands on hips, I poured the wine. I ordered it from Italy
because you said it was your favorite. I lit candles, bought
bedroom treasures and satin sheets I repeat. Where the hell
are you?

**I'M INDIGO: EVERYONE KNOWS MY NAME
MEANS BLUE**

CH.6
crown royal on ice

Panties off here we go
Let's take it nice and slow
Go for what you know
I am not a hoe
I like the way you flow
Bare breast in the air
Touch me I don't care
Visual so you stare
You ain't scared to take it there
Skin to skin and naked bare
You climb me like a stair
Reach my level if you dare
We can do it anywhere
How about right here in this chair
I'll lean over it if you ain't scared
Hold on a sec- let me say a prayer…

DEAR LORD,
I KNOW WE JUST MET BUT I THINK I'M IN LOVE FOR
REAL THIS TIME. PLEASE LET HIM LOVE ME BACK.
~ NEENAH

**NEENAH: MEANS RUNNING WATER, IMAGINE
THAT!**

CH.7
the evening you broke my heart

It was mad cold outside, I remember that because four hours later and after the fact, I ran outside into the winter air and jumped in my car. I drove 65 down a dark winding road, woke up my girl in the middle of the night screaming, "why doesn't anyone ever love me, why doesn't it stick, what is wrong with me?" But before we get to that, let me start at the beginning. I was so confused. As you said, you were the "inflictor". I don't know how you managed through this. Did you love me at all? Like for real, did you ever really love me?

You always called me Bae, or Babe, Baby, some form of sweet affection. But when you grabbed my hands and pulled me into you, and you called me by my whole name, not Santi, but Santiago, I knew that shit was about to blow up. I knew you were bowing out and so I screamed no, no, no! I said no, I threw your hands away from me, the tears began to fall. I couldn't breathe, I thought I was going to throw up my chest felt like it was caving in. You weren't prepared for my reaction, but you knew it would not be easy. Ironically, the whole time all I wanted was to take you in my arms, to kiss all of the confusion away. I wanted to place you inside of me and find our rhythm. Rhyme with you until your body shut down.

The parts that broke my heart

- I felt like you were untruthful, that you knew for quite some time that you started to feel differently about me~ that you didn't want to be with me (in a relationship) with me much longer than you admitted to.
- You said your feelings shifted near your daughters' birthday which was in the beginning of September. Even

if you said you were pushing yourself to work at "us", you still managed to little by little free yourself.

- I noticed the physical changes long before you admitted to it and don't think I didn't. You have no idea that turmoil that puts a woman through, especially a good woman holding it down for her man the way I did for you. I thought you were a man of integrity and you would share your heart. I thought maybe you were battling illness perhaps, had some stress with your family, kids, baby mama's and so I tried instead to reach out to you and you fucking pushed me away at every attempt.

- I felt unattractive, abandoned and dismissed by you when you denied my touch, my kisses, my offer of love.

- The last time I made love to you, you had sex with me. Everything felt different. Did you fake the orgasm as well? We only did it because I asked you. It was Christmas morning, and I had to ask you.

- I felt low after that. I wish you could have shared your heart, I expected that much from you based on who you said you were as a man.

- It broke my heart that during your time of "thought to transition out" you let me put my mouth on you. That's when you should have expressed your feelings, your truth. But instead, you let me blow you continuously and I did it out of love and a deep desire to please you. You received it without a whisper to me.

- I vomit at the thought of you allowing me to masturbate with you as my private audience, particularly the night before you destroyed my heart.

- You lied to my face three times the last time I came to your house. I asked you twice of you wanted "us" and you said yes! Then you told me you were too "tired- no energy to have your "sex"- my "love", but the next day when you ended it you said it was because you didn't want to continue taking my body knowing you felt however you felt. You said you've been frontin'!

- You suggested several times in answer form and on your own that you were interested in building a future with me. I believed your ass- why lie?
- Why say things you don't really mean like "I want to grow old with you"- are you fucking kidding me? That is so dirty and so irresponsible and immature! Who does that?

If I see you, I will ask and express my
QUESTIONS
1. Is my perception/perspective so far misconstrued?
2. Are you a fantastic liar?
3. Am I your enemy?
4. Why would you intentionally mislead and mistreat a person you call friend and claim to love and care about?
5. WHY ME?

CONCERNS
1. Friendship based on falsities?
2. Absolute clear communication.
3. Understanding your intentions.
4. Are you here solely because of your guilt?
5. I think your guilt should hurt you for days to come if you can't reconcile with your truth!

*** what your decision caused me ***
Severe depression
Weeks of sleepless nights having to self -medicate to sleep
Suicidal thoughts and feelings of nothingness
Questioning my judgement in men
Wondering if you were "the best of them", then what the hell does this mean?
Chest pains and too many tears
Isolation
Rage
Anger
A question of revenge
Three friendships now altered
Organize my thoughts, my mind, to write this

18

Dear Javier,

We made plans, an arrangement to speak face to
face and I had much to say. You invited my
conversation and said you wanted to be part of my
life and to be friends and I was trying to allow
myself to forgive you. I wanted mostly to resolve a
private situation in private. You accepted, but then
carelessly ruined my attempt at closure. Should
have listened to your girl when she told me to date
other people. Yep, she said that shit behind your
back but because she loves you, I guess and because
she swore you were one of the good guys. Not
messy, not young acting and aloof. I should have
read your song lyrics instead of just listening to
them. I wish you would have kept your word. If you
weren't lying about feeling guilty, then what is
about to come is really about to put something on
your mind. I should have stayed on mute! Oh my
god I hate you, I hate you and I don't even use this
language but, you know what Javier. Kill yourself!

*** what I know***

- If you have mean or hurtful things to say about me or to me, keep them to yourself.
- I held you at a certain standard. Not necessarily a pedestal, but in very high regard.
- I want my heart to be reassured that you aren't just another raggedy nigga rather than the king I've seen you as since I met you.
- Is that I love you and that will not cease.
- I pray you will never do this to another woman. Please don't!
- You made me believe it was safe to love again.
- You also caused me immeasurable pain that occasionally rises up and throat punches me.
- All of this, all of this bullshit caused me to write, so thank you. Even if everything I write is grief, death, hurt, desire, pain... I'm writing to heal the world, including myself.
- If I didn't have Jesus, not religion but Jesus, I would be dead.
- All of this is greater than you. Unfortunately, you were the catalyst, the fire-starter.
- I loved having you in my life
- I can't imagine life without you, I can't. I tried, it's hard, it's weird.
- I don't want to hate you.
- Music, mostly Sade helped me through this.

*** but now***

- What do you want from me?
- You said you want to be in my life still- but how? In what capacity? Are you even sure? I am. No! Hell, to the NO!
- A year and a half will pass. Something terrible will happen to me but I will survive, and you will finally man up and face me.
- Even in the thick of it, those first hours, days and months after it was over, I had to commend you for doing it face to face and not via text or over the phone. I had to speak my truth and say that even though you were not the man for me, you are still a really good man with a beautiful heart and a brilliant mind and when you are ready, when you're really ready, she will be the happiest woman on earth.

and all this love

Gave me thick skin, it heightened my discernment and broadened my horizons. This may have been the longest four-page letter of my life but, I think we learn the best lessons from pain and heartache. Years have passed and contrary to my belief back then, I did well learn how to be without you. Thank you for releasing me.

-Santi

HEY, I'M SANTI- MY NAME IS SHORT FOR SANTIAGO IT MEANS, "JAMES" IN SPANISH AND IN CASE YOU'RE WONDERING, I WAS NAMED AFTER MY DAD.

CH. ME
light skin -n- mocha all day

we often talked about love, the shape of it, the way to get it, how good it felt and how bad it hurt. We would debate about relationships and the quickest ways to get in and out of them and oh my God we loved music. We knew every song from every genre, we'd spend hours texting songs back and forth talking about "girl, that was my jam" and "ooh, wasn't nothing like the 80's, these millennials don't know shit, ooh they make me sick"! Then we'd fall out laughing. We'd talk about our years in the choir and why we didn't get more solo's and how we killed it at karaoke every single time! We were the coldest, we shared so much the way sisters do. I'm still angry, I still cry, I'm crying now because I want you to be here to share this, to see it, hold on, I can't breathe- I hate this!

okay, girl I hear your voice sometimes, I hear you singing, and I hear you laughing, and I look over my shoulder for you. It's like I'm bugging out. I hate every part of November 7th, 2018 for taking you away from this world, from your husband, your girls and grandbabies, all of your family and friends. I am in mourning even though I had a warning. I am filled with your love and laughter, even now the morning after. I never wanted to say good-bye for too many reasons why. Too soon your journey came to an end, I love you I love you my sister my friend. All I can do is stay busy, keep my mind occupied but every second of every day you're pretty much on my mind! I knew the phone call would come and I am definitely not the only one who is absolutely distraught about our current reality. My Beautiful sister, you said Heaven is where you wanted to be, pain-free and rejoicing," sanging in the heavenly choir" lol. Trying my best to honor you by being bold and brave and intentional and accomplishing my dreams. I wrote this for you. We promised to heal the world with our words, so...

10/15/18 9:10 am

I don't have much time to live sis they are putting me on hospice

YOU never could fit inside of a box, a label, or be tightly packaged, you are one extreme or the other, people either love you or love to hate you, so don't ask me to title this. Don't ask me to make this into something that it isn't or to pontificate. Don't ask me the purpose, the rhyme nor the reason. Don't ask me about ulterior motives, cycles or seasons. Do not ask me what this even is, what this will become and if these words will reach you.

I'M REACHING sis, haven't really slept since 10/15/18! Why did I have to wake up to that shit is what I have thought so many times, Why is this shit even happening is what the angry girl deep down inside is screaming, cussing actually but you and I both know that a temper tantrum from 44 year old me and dropping F-Bombs will not change that 46 year old you are facing death.

WE are Christians and so we will proclaim as we believe and stir up our faith...
God can do anything but FAIL!! They will call me crazy for eternity because I will never stop believing that he can do the impossible in you and through you! I continue to expect the miraculous and every day that you respond to my texts, answer my FaceTime's, I'm like **YOOOOO!!!** My sister is still here! The worse it gets, the more glory he gets when he flips this script. But you told me you were tired, you said you were ready for Heaven as hard as it was for you to come to this decision and I decided that I had to put on my big girl drawls and listen. I had to hear your heart. I had to accept the unacceptable, sing the un-sing-able.

I'M SELFISH SON, I learned that last Tuesday morning when you facetimed me from the hospital bed. The shit just got real **(If Mom reads this, she is gonna get my butt for cussing),** but you are my champion and you would stick up for me and say **"EH, MA…she gotta keep it real"!** and we would try to play it off without being mad disrespectful. Hell yeah, I'm selfish because you told me so and for so many other reasons. You told me I had to let you go and you especially knew how hard this would be and that's why you came and spent the week with me. JUST 3 weeks ago we sat on this couch eating pizza and laughing at POSE and NETFLIX flicks and laughing and singing and reminiscing and hollering and doing how we do US. You left on September 26th, 2018, a day before I turned 44. We are synchronized, we've been through too much and so I knew that I knew that you knew things were about to change, but the unspoken made it safe. Too bad the unspoken couldn't make it not real!

I'MMADASHELLCUZICAN'TMAKEITBETTER YOUAREALIVINGLEGENDLIVINGLARGE

THERE is too much to say, too much to sing, when I got engaged you were there when they sized my ring
You've held the umbrella over me through so many personal storms, we are connected
When haters came at me sideways and in between, just like a big sister, you
Protected
I still don't know what this is, an ode, a poem, a documentary, a song, a rap, a complimentary and eloquent dedication, to my big sister who rocked the worlds of every person she met, a speaker to the nations.

I KNOW NOW that the people you love the most are who you learn the most about life from. You are an epiphany, an ellipsis. So much more.

I'M ANGRY, I'm pissed off because I can't see your life as through…
But my name ain't JEHOVA or Christ so what am I supposed to do?
Just keep praying daily, really every minute
A thought doesn't enter my mind without you being in it, real talk!

I'M SELFISH because I made it all about me
It took days of weeping to God and talking to Mom to really get me to see
That YOU are the center of this situation, this ain't rocket science or a mathematic equation but what it is, is, a testament of your character, the strength of your faith, the beauty of your smile, the swing in your hip, the journey walked in miles and miles of adversity, celebration, overcoming and determination
How can I not smile about your legacy, the one existing currently?

IF I COULD, MAIL MY HEART RIGHT TO YOU I WOULD…
I'D PACK IT UP, SEAL IT TIGHT AND I'D SEND IT OVERNIGHT…

LYRICS from our favorite song. We were so COLD singing that at Karaoke and at my Graduation party! The world can't stop us, they never could!

LIGHTSKIN, how Blessed am I to have been given the privilege of being your little sister. You are one of the greatest treasures of my heart. So much of who I am, who I desire to become has been strongly impacted by the example you have given. All the things we discussed regarding our purpose and what we've spoken into this universe, I promise to stay in the race. I will get these books published. I pray

that we can grow old together, travel the nations and tell the world about Jesus and the miracles that are OUR LIVES
I pray that I have shown you love both unconditionally and the love of Christ.

HOW do I end this? How do I end? Do I press delete or do I press save and send?
ALL I know is, don't PUSH ME, CUZ I'M CLOSE TO THE EDGE, AND I'M TRYING NOT TO LOSE MY HEAD, HUH, HUH, UHN, UHN, UHN
IT'S LIKE A JUNGLE SOMETIMES IT MAKES ME WONDER HOW I KEEP FROM GOING UNDER
REAL TALK

I guess this is a letter?
Maybe this is a spoken word piece that I will finally perform on stage like we talked about?
Could this be a monologue?
What is this? Girl I don't know, all I do know is that it was burning my insides and I had to get it out. Your liver is swollen today, and I am feeling empathy pains. Perhaps the title of this is *SONG FOR MY SISTER, SISTERSONG, LATASHA-LATASHA*

I'LL holla light skin and if you do move to heaven, please send me some form of confirmation that Jesus is in fact Puerto Rican/Dominican and Black…he's mixed basically!!

I love you forever-xoxo
eightnineteenpm tentwentyfoureighteen

LATASHA: MEANS "BIRTH OF CHRIST"
IT MAKES SO MUCH SENSE NOW

I AM, N'KYENGE AYANNA: MEANS
BRILLIANT FIRSTBORN
AKA MOCHA CHOCOLATTE

26

CH. 8: PUT THE NEEDLE ON THE RECORD

LET'S LOVE
LET'S MOTIVATE
LET'S LIFT HIGH
LET'S DANCE
LET'S FORGET ABOUT OUR TROUBLE
LET'S RUN IN THE RAIN
LET'S APPRECIATE
LET'S PRESERVE
LET'S MULTIPLY
LET'S INVOKE PEACE
LET'S CATCH AND RELEASE
LET'S MAKE LOVE UNTIL WE'RE BREATHLESS
LET'S PASSION
LET'S OCEAN
LET'S RIVER NILE
LET'S WAIT AWHILE
LET'S NINA SIMONE
LET'S BE ALONE
LET'S GET IT ON
LET'S QUIET STORM
LET'S LOVE
LET'S L.O.V.E. LOVE

MY NAME IS MAGDALENA, IN A BIBLICAL SENSE,
IT MEANS OF MAGDAL BUT IT IS ALSO A RIVER IN
COLUMBIA THAT FLOWS INTO THE CARIBBEAN.
KINDA LIKE ME, I JUST FLOW.

CH. 9
Bars verses lyrics: Love-song-cento

Afro flows
High floating
Like milky way clouds
Reminiscent of
Butterscotch colored skin
She switches
And she struts
Slowly but surely
One foot in front of the
Other
She's strictly business
He's strictly dictation
Talking all that talk
She-she wants sincerity
Stability and romance
She keeps walking
Sandals clicking
Mini skirt tipping from
Side to side
As curvaceous undertones and fully structured thighs rise
high
To the occasion
Ah shucks, I think we have a situation
Her afro flows
Nappy, curly and full
Burnt orange mango and
Sanded brown
She's ready to get down
Brown like the freckles that decorate her face
She's worth it, she's worth it
She does not belong to anyone but
Chicago is her space and her place in time
She-kah-go! her silky voice can send you to the moon
And her lyrics will blow your mind

She is my sunshine afro sister
Perfect melody of natural and essence
She stands tall like heaven
Fingers and toes painted to perfection
But she won't leave marks on the wall
Or scratches on his back
You can find her in silence and
Learn that is when she speaks the most
Between tongue kisses and eyelashes curled
Love unfurls- thank God her
Afro flows like
Blues and jazz Indigo
And deep-down neo-soul
And Sunday dinner soul food
Floating out the window
She is sending I miss you
It's getting really personal
I miss you
I'm traveling miles I have no comprehension of
Absolutely, I am closing my eyes trying desperately
Not to lust after love seriously
I am telling the truth always and never
Minding shades of gray
But still keeping it real and crisp and clean like the white
linen palazzo pants I continue to imagine you wearing I am
not accepting the notion of a friendship stolen by inaccurate
timing, I am keeping close tabs on my spirituality and walk
with he so that all can be right for you to come to me.
I am
At times mixed up, I'm challenged to give up knowing that
if I gave up this beauty would never come to pass, and I am
looking far ahead to unknown places. I'm seeing the smiles
on my babies faces and nothing in this world could feel
much better accept perhaps your fingers intertwined with
mine
Unifying us we become one black fist, we must
Maintain our power and strength

Oh baby, can't you see it
We are Black Art
Folks spending all they dollars for fragments of us!
My afro flows into
This skin we are in
This blessing on which we depend
I am missing you in a distant land
I am petitioning Jesus to cause you to understand and for
myself as well, to understand and I am realizing that we
taught each other very well and too well to forget
We are light and at the end of the night before the end of
the day
We did not know each other at all...

I am saving and surviving and sparing my friendship for
you
I am remembering your voice
Your eyes
Your lips
Your words spoken eloquently and clearly
Ghetto sophisticated and so very real to me
I am wondering if you will become my other half
I am wondering if you will give me that chocolate little boy
that my mama saw in her dream, she said I called him
Gabriel
Well

My mind stays frazzled as patience is not my virtue, I'm
questioning myself and possibly my sanity thinking you
and I are meant to be
I have loved you possibly without even knowing you
stayed inside of my soul and held me tight from the inside

N'Kyenge Ayanna

You make me feel sexy, like mad
Sexy are my full lips painted to perfection, I
Am the lady in red patiently awaiting your chocolate kisses
dipped in moonlight- yeah, that's some good stuff you say
and close your eyes for some more and I flirtatiously walk
away

Sexy is us, I am always thinking about us now
Amel Larrieux hums and sings and quenches her thirst and
I am every high note in this duet
We are acapella dreaming, we are serenading,
Dancing in evening shadows and
Candle light flickers

Your chocolate covered strawberry kisses taste
Cool in my mouth, right now
I'm standing in front of you, I'm
Intimately smiling, I'm ready
Because I am not afraid, of this serial monogamy this
affection erogenous emancipation baby
This is not another love song
This is love.

MY NAME'S CATI (KAH-TEE): SHORT FOR
CATALINA-MY NAME MEANS PURE

CH. 10: THE B SIDE

The air was mad thick, it felt like you were swallowing the sun it was so freaking hot, but the streets were poppin' and everyone styled to impress in their summertime fits, and she was no different, an implant from Chicago on vacation to visit her little sister Magdalena. She sashayed down 59th and 4th to hit up Rosa's Bakery which had the best tacos and she promised herself to indulge in as many of the spots her little sis raved about in their weekly Facetime chats.

Yeah, it was mad hot, but you would hear no complaints from Indigo because she was in Brooklyn, oh yeah, the **BROOK- TO- THE- LYN** and this trip would prove beneficial on multiple levels. She had every moment accounted for on her variation of lists. She made lists for everything, it was the way her world worked. She would have sister time with Lena, possibly expose some family secrets, mend some bridges and dig up some ancestral roots, she needed to know where she came from. She was so here for it, *all of it*. The ambiance, the food, the foolery and getting in some firsthand research for her book.

They hadn't grown up there, but their father shared stories of his youth in New York and his fathers' migration from the Islands to first Brooklyn and finally settling in Spanish Harlem where his life would be taken to soon and his family would be left behind devastated and suffering for generations to come.

She steps into a puddle and feels the splash attack her toes, ankle and mid-calf. She reaches down to her bare leg to push away the inconvenience and to check if her favorite mustard yellow Chuck Taylor sandals were damaged. Luckily, they weren't, and she wouldn't have to pretend to not be affected greatly. She wasn't even a materialistic person, but her struggle with OCD would have caused her to track all the way back to Lena's apartment. Lena still allowed Indigo and their Mom to call her Lena but insisted that everyone else she encountered call her by Magdalena, she was militant and impossible that way. Nobody knows when and how she got that way but loved her all the same.

The candles burned
The moon went down
The polished hill
The milky town
Transparent, weightless, luminous
Uncovering the two of us
On that fundamental ground
Where love's unwilled, unleashed,
Unbound
And half the perfect world is found

She loved Madelyn Peyroux and she tried to just hum it when the song populated on her Astrud Gilberto station on Pandora, but she couldn't. Before she knew it, her pacing slowed, and her sashay became a sexy slow -motion soliloquy. Her hips controlling every word, every vibration of the melody singing in her ear. She couldn't hold it in anymore, she belted out as she floated down the block almost passing up Rosa's Bakery.

As she walked in, she lifted on her tippy-toes looking for Lena but didn't see her. She was starving but had a thing about appointments and beginning without the other person, it was bad ju-ju. "Lena, donde estas?" she texted, ""I'm here"! She clicked on the notes section of her I-phone, clicked on the microphone and began to dictate in a soft voice –

bloodied water floating sin
brown cheeks smashed against porcelain
know hurt worse
than empty ness
no rest for tenderness
of Brazilian breasts, amazon-ish and sunken

squirting tears for the tomorrow that will never come
She was just about to correct all of the grammatic typos
courtesy of her iphone when she got a text alert; "tres
minutos nena- RELAX ☺ "! She couldn't help but smile,
she and Lena were very close, and she didn't want any
drama on this trip.

They were both grieving the recent passing of their father,
but Lena was taking it the hardest, Daddy's youngest
princess as she was affectionately called. She had been
attending a non-traditional support group for grieving
women that used a combined effort of Art and Music
therapy in efforts to heal and begin to adjust to life without
their loved ones.

It was Lena's idea to meet for taco's before she took her
sister to some must see spots in Brooklyn. She was excited
because Indigo agreed to go to her Grieve Group with her
and because she knew her sister and her OCD tendencies,
she figured she'd at least give her a heads up. Some of the
women could be long winded, loss brought stuff out of you
and she didn't want her to become irritated and take away
from the marvelous work the group was doing. They were
sweet and Lena didn't want her to lose sight of that.

They passed through Sunset Park, the smell of ganja or
(reefer) as the old heads called it, perfumed the air. They
walked briskly, stepping over needles on the way to the N
train on 4th avenue thankful it was still daylight. They knew
better than to pass by the abandoned warehouses that would
soon be turned into luxurious condos. Whispers from
generations of folk who were the very bricks of Brooklyn
consumed the neighborhoods. Gentrification escapes no
man.

Indigo was reminded of the yellow brick road as the
hallway walls were painted a sunshine yellow, not a

mustard yellow but bright ass sunshine. She tried not to be critical but couldn't help but tease her sister. "Come on and ease on down, ease on down the road"! she sang in her best Diana Ross impression. They fell into each other laughing. It felt so good to be together, to be sisters up close instead of millions of miles away.

The room was set up, it was beautiful actually and Indigo found herself very impressed. The décor was a mixture of Bohemian and Afrocentric with a very expensive color palate and high-end finishes. They really spent a lot of time and money on this place she thought. Just then, Lena said, Yani owns this entire building, her offices are through the back and down the hall, she laid this place out didn't she!

They stepped inside of the circle, each woman greeting the other with a warm embrace before sitting. Yani stood up first and welcomed everyone. Indigo felt herself becoming anxious, not knowing what to expect, Lena grabbed her hand causing her to look at her sister with slight embarrassment. Her eyebrows perched and she began the silent conversation with her Sister. What the hell is this? Are we about to chant or something?

Her sister smiled back, her slanted green eyes were calming just like their mothers. All of the women joined hands and had a moment of silence for the loved ones they lost. That was the whole purpose of the group, no, it wasn't weird or qwerky, it wasn't some new black cult. Just nine women who had one common denominator, and wasn't that enough?

Santi, the woman seated to the left of Indigo was admiring her sandals and complimented her before handing her the stack of leather-bound journals and pens to circulate. Indigo smiled and said thank you politely then reached in her purse to discretely squeeze a few drops of hand sanitizer, she had that dirty germ sensation. She used her own pen.

Before we share today, I want to flip the script a little bit and change the order of things. Indigo, you are certainly welcome to participate in everything we do here, we do want you to feel comfortable and a part of the group.

Indigo smiled. Yani began to write a prompt on the white board with her summer mango manicured finger. She was breath-taking. The room looked more like a modeling convention then a grief therapy group.

I D E N T I T Y
- *Unpack this as freely as you can!*
- *Who are you?*
- *Can you be defined?*
- *What does your name mean?*
- *If your name does not have meaning, what would you want it to mean?*

Yani stood at the white board poised but soft. She folded her hands across her waist, resting them in the middle of her washboard belly. What I want is for us to try to begin to have the conversation about who we are but more importantly, who we are without those that we lost.

What is love to you in this moment? What is your story, your thoughts, your tomorrow? Please share in any written form of your choosing and at the end, be sure to write your name and the meaning. We'll discuss at the end of group.

She twisted off the cap of a Ting and took a modest sip. Alexa, play Jill Scott please! Jill would set the mood to spill it all on the page. She sat down and crossed her legs.

N'Kyenge Ayanna

Dear James,

I hope this letter finds you well. I really do mean that, I
hope it reaches you in the best of health. I'm certain your
right hand is palming your chest in shock. It has been quite
some time since we've spoken, years in fact. I was tempted
to begin this letter with an ode that began "My Ebony
Padre"; I get tickled every time I imagine you saying that in
baritone. I trust you are critiquing my grammar and I would
bet a pot of Spaghetti that you're paying much too close
attention to my diction/language and syntax making sure
that I don't break any rules. I smile at the prediction.

I'm sorry that this isn't a poem or maybe it is, or it will be
by the end because I think it's like you said, "The poetry is
in me". I know, I'm breaking your heart…right? So,
Santiago, you've been in my thoughts and we should talk,
seriously.

There are some things I think you should know. I'll try hard
to stay focused because you know I write the way I talk,
and we do not have time for all that. First you should know
that my mother and I traveled to the Dominican Republic
this past June and it was amazing. Unfortunately, when I
got back to the states, my job was terminated. The most
devastating pat which I'm sure you're digesting right now
is the loss of medical insurance. Keep reading, do not pick
up the phone! I'm serious Daddy, don't.

I want you to know that I'm embracing life and I'm always
up for a challenge. No worries, my Mom says God is in
control and I believe her. I know you feel the same way.
Anyway, I take my meds sparingly so only on the days that
I really can't function. I've been doing well up until last
week. It was crazy, I became so ill I had to leave school
twice. It scared me and I don't want to be scared. It really

put my mind to work. I thought about life and love and acceptance and I do not want this to be the end of me. I thought about you. A lot.

I also don't want you to be sick and living on borrowed time. I don't want you to leave yet. I want to get better so I can live my life and I want to give you yours back. The little girl in me needs this to happen. I was playing Asha the other day and something about her smile gave me hope. It made me feel like it's already all right and I wanted to share that with you.

No worries Sugar, we will be fine!
I know your smiling Daddy.

So much love,

Santi

N'Kyenge Ayanna

Mom

the grass patch cushioned
my fears

from staccato solo steps
to stiletto stretched runways

I knew every moment
of her smile

waiting patiently, always

extended arms
and Chloe scented neck hugs

my very first love
you lead, I will follow

I love you more than enough...

So like I know I talk way too much and I always have something to say and sometimes I totally have a tendency to just ramble on and on and you know I can make a long story longer but the thing is honey-baby, I so need to tell you something and I just can't find the words. Oh my God I totally love you, I'm so serious I love you, I really do. I've loved you my whole life actually at least that is the way it seems I mean that is the way that I feel, and I know our love is solid and you love me too. So, like we have this amazing history together and I've been your forever lover for ten, wife for six and mother to your children for four- and that counts for everything, it means something! So sweetheart, there is no easy way to say this, but this last one may not be yours. The thing is, when too lost your job, like I became so totally frustrated and I felt so much pressure and we really weren't communicating, we weren't in sync and it was difficult, and I felt angry, but I swear to God baby I did not intentionally betray you. I never ever thought I would cheat on you. It didn't mean anything, it didn't. He was my first and a friend and I only wanted someone to talk to and he agrees it was a mistake. He swore to tell his wife and I promised to tell you because we both realize our indiscretion and we regret it and I just have to fix this mess I created! I have to fix it because I love you, I love you so much. Don't worry, nobody in the family knows. The only person I told was Semaj and she told me to tell you right away, but I couldn't, I was afraid of losing you. Just know that you are my world and I love you more than enough and I guess if you're reading this letter, I'm already gone.

N'Kyenge Ayanna

THE RING

secrets
told
 and
kept
with
lips
locked
throat
swallows
that
choke.
forever
promises
decorated
on
paper
slowly
tarnish
while
love
circles
 the
ring
no
longer
two
now
three

BLACK JESUS PERSONIFIED

I see you in silhouette

dreds become hung

rope like and I'm

hanging at the tips

of these

shea-buttered snakes

hissing at my confusion

what does it all mean?

Egyptian musk slippery

oil stretched wide over my creativity

and I cannot get you outta my Zen-

think me another thought thanks

for the conscious memory

FOUND GUILTY (REMIX)

So, it's like this
and I know I'm full of words usually and I'm always
running my mouth but this time
the words aint comin'
I can't hardly find them

So, it's like this
I love you and everything
like that I love you
for real. I have
all my life
and we share mad love for each other
right?

and I'm not just your chick on the side
I'm your wife. Been your wife
for six years lover for ten
baby's mama for five
I really do love you   but
this last one might not belong to you

when you weren't working, I was stressed and
I accidentally stepped out on you
he was my fist and a friend I just needed to talk to
I never in my life thought I'd ever cheat on you

the   seed   was   planted   within   a   week   of
consummation
so, I'm trippin' on if the daddy is him or you

I'm still the same person that fell in love with you
I love you still and I want to be real with you
he agreed to tell his wife if I agreed to tell you
but the baby doesn't look like him he looks like you
the only person I told was Semaj, she told me to tell
you
from the jump but I couldn't
until now and if you're reading this
I must be gone
I'm sorry

Life in the Raw
I am celebrating me
The virgin-ess of me
The parts they've never seen
I'm closing the dark and opening the light
Three more sips and life is a cocktail
I am dreaming while I'm awake
I keep my secrets to myself
I'm giving more than I can take
I shake my convictions out the back door
If somebody really loves you, they'll come
back for more
Three more sips and life is a cocktail
Life presumes to fake me
The mirror attempts to escape me but
I feel the smooth of my skin, then
I realize I'm dying all over again
Three more sips and life is a cocktail

SOUL HAIKU

Afro pick brown lips
Kiss my cheeks puddinpop Dad
You were my hero

Slick hustler blacksnake
Slithered life away from US
No money or food

Little girls hold hands
Afro puffs to piggy tails
Best friends see no race

Brilliant first-born girl
N'Kyenge Ayanna Brown
You're unique, not weird

Shake a tail feather
Pluck my soul if tonight sleeps
Love sits in my lap

Breathe sigh inhale lie
Still no smoke love dust lingers
Time pissed on my clock

Brown hips white thigh highs
Blue eyes gaze back to brown love
Crayon box melts truth

Nassau pride no hide
Slanted eyes cheek bones high
Yea mon, fish peas rice

N'Kyenge Ayanna

From poetry's womb
Chocolate skin color and taste
Spice of life cooks freedom

Jill Scott and Lauryn
Hill are the dopest singers
Lyrical masters

Diallo Telli
My brother bold warrior
God speak, he will listen

I got three brown babes
Asha Khalil and Noah
They love me for real

Khalilah Yasmeen
Dopest chocolate on the scene
She's my sister Yo!

Mom you're my best friend
Confident, homie, my girl
I love when you smile

untitled

I saw him with slanted eyes
I saw him straight forward
aesthetically pleasing
as much as he allows me to see
he is the most beautiful masculine melody I have
ever heard
I become his audience
he smiles, is he
aware of my affection, I reach for my journal
because he has inspired me to poetry
then the train comes and
we get on
he turns left
and disappears
right-

I'm calling this one my Zen within

Undeniably
unaware of my Zen within
my internal journey
what is this crap
I'm on my way to external bliss
thinking about the last time we kissed
what have I missed?
what have I missed?
creativity I recognized
with my poetry I got baptized
and became brand new art
again
unaware of my Zen
up until now and way back then
I may have cursed it at the root
ground it up and smoked it then
played it like my flute
instrumental
in this mediation of life
I may have denied it
was petrified of it
classified it with buddah
and not the funky lounge
I sit silent and surreal serious
I look, I dig
I find my Zen through the ink of my pen
and I become undeniably
aware of my Zen within
I accept it
in the name of art

I'm not lying, I can't make this up

Love ain't shit
I heard this lady say that in church
I wondered if she was drunk but
I don't think she was, I
think she was hurting inside
I think she had enough or too much
maybe she was ruined
maybe her shoes were too tight
it had to be something
it's always something
I was walking down Wabash, trying to catch the
blue line, lost somehow
A random man who belonged to the streets shouted
at me and suddenly we were the only people in
Chicago
he said
Love ain't shit
I thought I was being punked
I started walking sideways
scared as all get out
that's why they call me chicken
I don't even eat meat, but they still call me chicken
and
I ran all the way to Michigan Ave.
took out my phone to call an uber, I
got a text from him
three years ago, him
talkin' about he loves me
are you kidding me?
Love aint shit!

Thank you so much for reading. I hope you enjoyed the experience of **THIS IS NOT ANOTHER LOVE SONG**. Please look out for future works by N'Kyenge Ayanna. Follow my social media outlets
FaceBook : Author/Poetress N'Kyenge Ayanna,
Instagram: @nkyengeayanna,
Twitter: @NKYENGEAYANNA, and my blog at www.eyeamnkyengeayanna.blogspot.com.

Made in the USA
Lexington, KY
26 May 2019